NIGERIA

Mary N. Oluonye

Lerner Publications Company • Minneapolis

Lerner Publications Company
A division of Lerner Publishing Group, Inc.
241 First Avenue North
Minneapolis, MN 55401 U.S.A.

Website address: www.lernerbooks.com

Library of Congress Cataloging-in-Publication Data

Oluonye, Mary N.
    Nigeria / by Mary N. Oluonye.
        p.   cm. — (Country explorers)
    Includes index.
    ISBN 978-0-8225-7131-5 (lib. bdg. : alk. paper)
    1. Nigeria—Juvenile literature. 2. Nigeria—Social life and customs—
Juvenile literature. I. Title.
    DT515.22.O49 2008
    966.9—dc22   2006035846

Manufactured in the United States of America
2 – VI – 11/1/10

Table of Contents

Welcome!

Nigeria is a big country on the western coast of the continent of Africa. Nigeria is shaped kind of like a square. The countries of Niger and Chad lie at the top, or north, of the square. Benin sits to Nigeria's left, or west. To the right, or east, is Cameroon. The Gulf of Guinea forms Nigeria's bottom, or southern side. The gulf is part of the Atlantic Ocean.

Nigeria

Nigerians enjoy a sunny day at a sandy beach along the Gulf of Guinea.

4

ATLANTIC OCEAN

NIGER

CHAD

LAKE CHAD

Argungu

SOKOTO RIVER

Kano

NIGERIA

BENIN

LAKE KAINJI

Abuja ★

NIGER RIVER

BENUE RIVER

CAMEROON

Lokoja

NIGER RIVER

MILES
0   200

0   200
KILOMETERS

Lagos

NIGER DELTA

GULF OF
GUINEA

5

rain forest
coastal zone
savanna
plateau
mountains
country's capital
city

The Land

Kids from southern Nigeria can play on the beaches along the coast. Some kids might take a trip to the tropical rain forests in the south. These wet, green forests provide homes for gorillas, chimpanzees, monkeys, forest elephants, and more.

Thick, green rain forests cover parts of southern Nigeria.

In the middle of the country, kids can run through big, grassy fields called savannas. Children in the dry and dusty north have fun too. This area is not far from the Sahara. People in that desert still travel around on camels!

Camels reach for leaves growing on trees in the dry north.

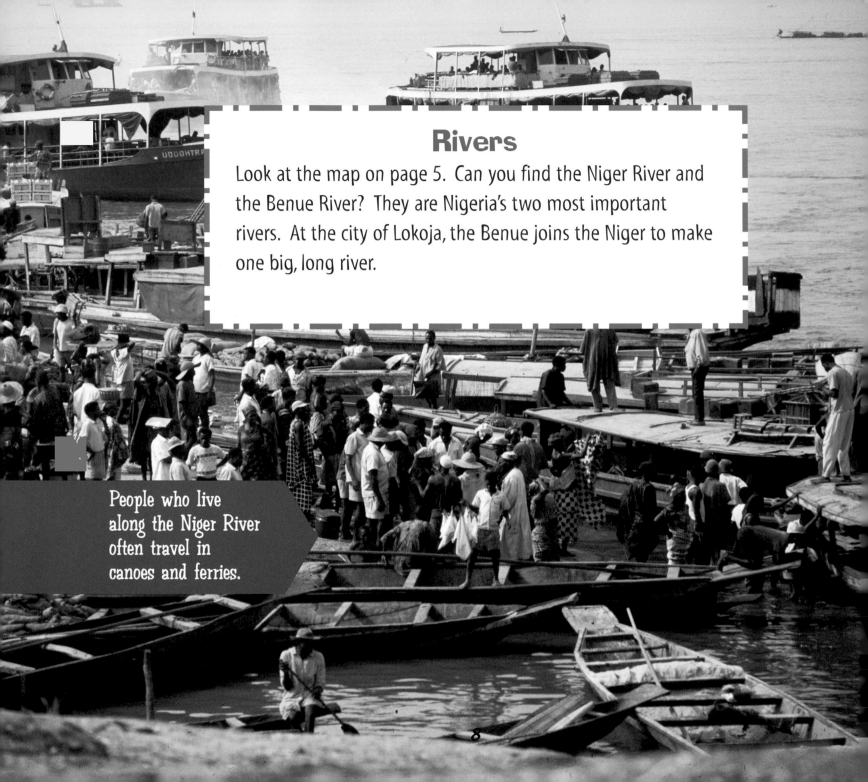

Rivers

Look at the map on page 5. Can you find the Niger River and the Benue River? They are Nigeria's two most important rivers. At the city of Lokoja, the Benue joins the Niger to make one big, long river.

People who live along the Niger River often travel in canoes and ferries.

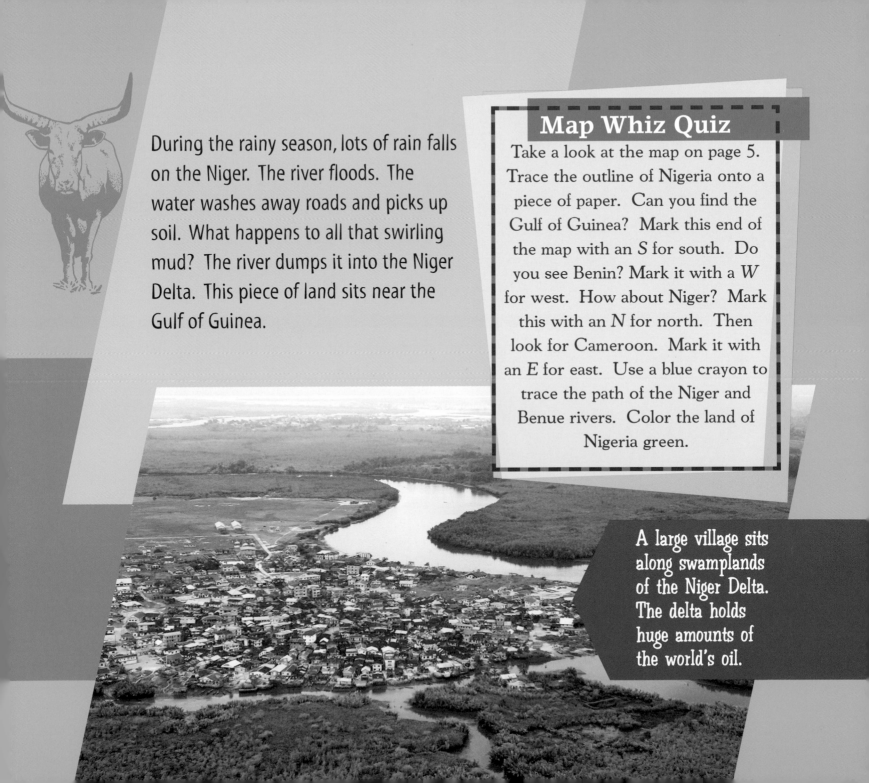

During the rainy season, lots of rain falls on the Niger. The river floods. The water washes away roads and picks up soil. What happens to all that swirling mud? The river dumps it into the Niger Delta. This piece of land sits near the Gulf of Guinea.

Map Whiz Quiz

Take a look at the map on page 5. Trace the outline of Nigeria onto a piece of paper. Can you find the Gulf of Guinea? Mark this end of the map with an *S* for south. Do you see Benin? Mark it with a *W* for west. How about Niger? Mark this with an *N* for north. Then look for Cameroon. Mark it with an *E* for east. Use a blue crayon to trace the path of the Niger and Benue rivers. Color the land of Nigeria green.

A large village sits along swamplands of the Niger Delta. The delta holds huge amounts of the world's oil.

A Fulani girl carries a decorated pot on her head.

People

A long time ago, different groups of people ruled parts of Nigeria. Each group had its own language, religion, and history. Two major groups, the Hausa and the Fulani, lived in the north. The Yoruba lived in the southwest. The Igbo lived in the southeast.

In the 1800s, a powerful European country called Great Britain took over all the land. The British named the area Nigeria, after the big river. In 1960, the British left. The people of Nigeria again ruled the country.

Say What?

Like the British, most Nigerians speak English. It is the country's official language. Nigerians use English at school and at work. At home, people like to speak their own Nigerian language. They might speak Hausa, Yoruba, Igbo, or one of Nigeria's five hundred other languages.

Students celebrate Nigeria's independence on October 1, 1960.

Hausa often decorate their homes with colorful patterns and shapes. This house is in the city of Kano.

Up North

Both the Hausa and the Fulani live north of the Niger and Benue rivers. The Hausa have farmed and traded in northern Nigeria for a long time. They grow rice, fruits, and vegetables.

A Fulani man moves his zebus across the savanna.

Many Fulani move from place to place. They look for water and food for the animals they raise. Other Fulani live in Nigeria's cities.

Down South

Most Yoruba live in southwestern Nigeria. Many fish or farm for a living. Some Yoruba farmers grow cacao beans. The beans are used to make chocolate.

This Yoruba woman and her daughter live in the city of Lagos.

14

The Igbo make their homes in the southeast. When the British first came to Nigeria, they hired the Igbo for important jobs. The Igbo started to live like the British. These days, many Igbo are doctors, lawyers, or traders.

Three Igbo women in traditional clothing pose for a photo.

Stay Cool!

Do you put on shorts when it is hot outside? Nigerian kids do too. But they also wear traditional clothes. Nigerian men and boys wear caps and long robes over loose pants. The clothes are made of a thin cloth that keeps people cool.

These Yoruba men are wearing long, wide robes called *agbadas*.

Village girls show off their brightly colored clothing.

Each group wears different colors. Hausa men like white. Fulani men like light yellow or blue. Yoruba men like patterns, and Igbo men like dark red.

Northern women wear robes and head coverings. Yoruba and Igbo women and girls wear long, colorful skirts, shirts, and head scarves.

Villages and Cities

Where do you live? Most Nigerians live in villages and towns. Their houses are made of wood or mud. There is usually no electricity. And there are no indoor bathrooms.

People in this Yoruba village built their homes out of wood.

Nigeria's cities are crowded. Many city dwellers live in high-rise apartment buildings. Lagos, in southern Nigeria, is the biggest city. Traffic jams are so bad they are called go-slows.

Kano is a northern city. It has a new section and an old section. Most Hausa live in the Old City. Its huge mud walls were built long ago to protect the Hausa from attackers.

Cars and buses make their way through downtown Lagos.

Family

In Nigeria, mothers, fathers, brothers, sisters, grandparents, aunts, uncles, and cousins are all part of one, big extended family. In small towns and villages, an extended family shares a group of houses called a compound. There are always other kids around to play with! All grown-ups take turns watching the kids.

This is a Hausa compound.

All in the Family

Here are some Hausa words for family members.

grandfather	kaka	(kah-KAH)
grandmother	kakani	(kah-kah-NEE)
uncle	kawu	(kah-WOO)
aunt	iya	(EE-yah)
father	uba	(oo-BAH)
mother	uwa	(oo-WAH)
son	yaro	(YAH-roh)
daughter	yarinya	(yah-RIN-yah)
brother	dan'uwa	(dan-OO-wah)
sister	'yar'uwa	(yar-OO-wah)

A family in
Lagos poses
for a portrait.

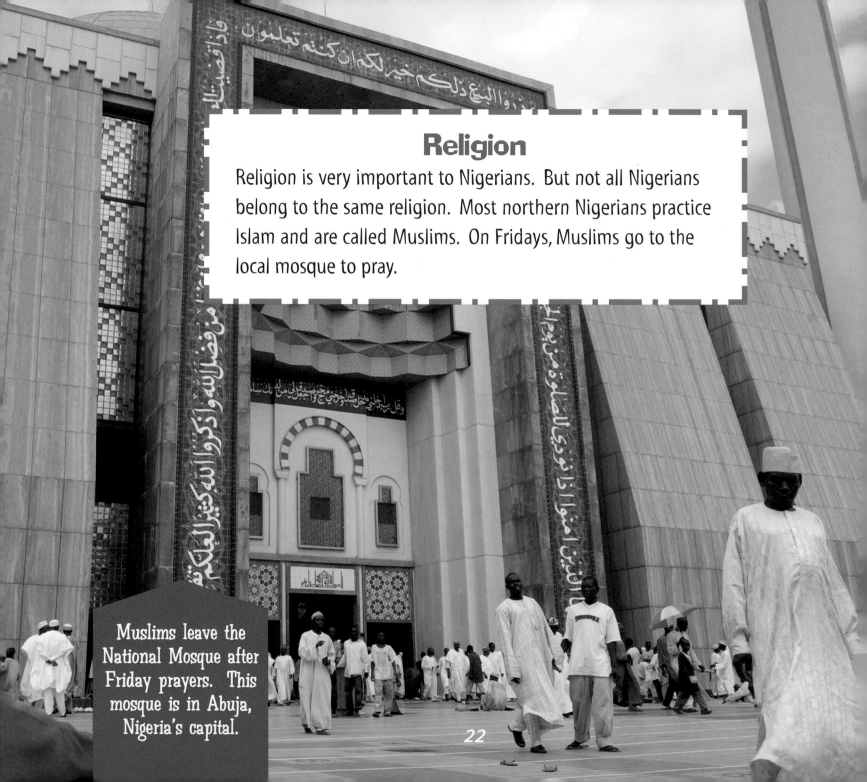

Religion

Religion is very important to Nigerians. But not all Nigerians belong to the same religion. Most northern Nigerians practice Islam and are called Muslims. On Fridays, Muslims go to the local mosque to pray.

Muslims leave the National Mosque after Friday prayers. This mosque is in Abuja, Nigeria's capital.

22

Most Christians live in the south. In Nigerian churches, the prayer leader says the Sunday service in English. Then another person says it in a local Nigerian language.

Many Nigerians also practice traditional African religions. They pray to many different gods. Sometimes, they ask dead relatives for help with problems.

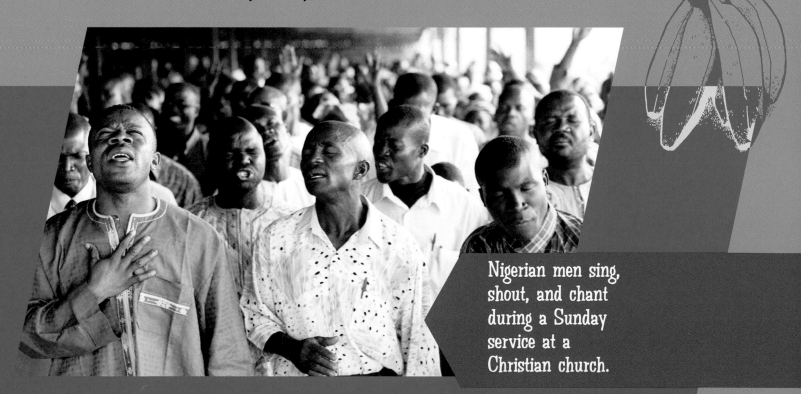

Nigerian men sing, shout, and chant during a Sunday service at a Christian church.

23

Names

After a baby is born, family and friends have a naming party. In Yoruba families, the oldest family member prays for the new baby and sprinkles the child's mouth with honey, water, and salt. The honey is for the good times in the child's life. The water is supposed to bring greatness. The salt is for the hard times in life.

A Nigerian man holds his newborn child.

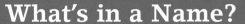
What's in a Name?

Ada	(ah-DAH)	Igbo for "first daughter"
Jumoke	(joo-MOH-keh)	Yoruba for "everyone loves the child"
Kehinde	(KEN-day)	Yoruba for "second born of twins"
Taiye	(TIE-yay)	Yoruba for "first born of twins"
Uzoamaka	(oo-zo-a-MAH-kah)	Igbo for "the way is good"

All the guests put the mixture on their tongues too. The oldest family member calls out the baby's name. Everyone repeats the name. The ceremony ends with a big party. How did you get your name?

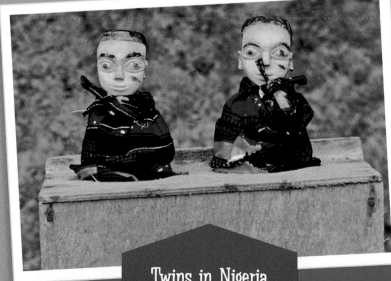

Twins in Nigeria are celebrated. Many Nigerians think twins are special gifts from God.

Celebrate!

Nigerians celebrate many events throughout the year. Some festivals happen when Nigerians gather food.

In Igbo towns and villages, people have a yam party. When the yams are ready to be harvested, villagers get together to celebrate. Cooks boil, roast, or fry yams to make tasty Nigerian dishes. Everyone eats lots of yams, dances, and plays games.

A farmer pulls yams out of the ground. Yams look kind of like long potatoes.

26

The town of Argungu holds a fishing festival once a year. Thousands of men and boys wade into the Sokoto River carrying nets. They use the nets to try to scoop up the biggest fish.

Nigeria

Hi Mom & Dad!

I'm having fun here in Nigeria. Today, Grandpa and I went to watch the Argungu Fishing Festival. It's the only time when people are allowed to fish in the river. That's too bad because some people were catching really big fish! Later, we watched dancing and wrestling. The wrestling matches are a pretty big deal. Boys come from other villages to compete. The winners get prizes.

See you soon!

Your F

Your

Anywhe

School

When Nigerian kids turn six years old, they start school. In Nigeria, students wear uniforms to class. The school day lasts from 8:00 to 1:00. School is fun, but it is also hard work. After school, kids must do their homework before they can play.

A Nigerian girl and boy study together at school.

28

Young children sing during a school assembly.

Every few years, students have to take a big exam. If they pass, they can go to the next level of school.

The Market

Bananas here! Red-hot peppers for sale! Most Nigerians buy their food at outdoor markets. Markets are great places to buy fresh fruits and vegetables, meat, fish, cloth, pottery, and almost everything else. Everyone tries to get the best price. Even children learn to bargain. The market is also a fun spot to chat with friends.

Food sits out at a market in the northeastern city of Bauchi.

Bargaining

Buyer: How much is that bunch of bananas?

Seller: Two dollars.

Buyer: No, I'm sorry, but I can't pay two dollars for them. (The buyer starts to walk away.)

Seller: Okay, customer, come back. How much do you want to pay for them?

Buyer: One dollar.

Seller: Give me $1.50.

Buyer: How about $1.25? That's all I can pay.

Seller: Okay, okay.

A man sells carrots at a Nigerian street market.

Lunch is on! These Nigerian women prepare food over fires.

Food

Yeow! Drink plenty of milk during a Nigerian dinner because the food is hot! A popular dish is pepper soup. This thick, spicy soup is eaten with boiled cassava or yams.

After the cassava or yams are pounded, they look and taste a little like mashed potatoes. Nigerians roll a bit of the mashed cassava or yam into a ball. Then, they dip it into the soup and pop it into their mouths.

This Nigerian meal includes goat stew, peanuts, yams, and cooking bananas called plantains.

Artwork

Long ago, Nigerian artists made sculptures out of metal, wood, or ivory. Carving and sculpting are still popular. These days, artists carve wood to make the masks that dancers wear at festivals. Some artists carve pictures to tell stories. Artists sell their work at the market, in shops, or even by the roadside.

Women use hot pieces of iron to carve designs onto calabash gourds.

In Kano, artists make beautiful cloth in dye pits. They take white cloth and soak it in dyes made from indigo plants. The cloth becomes a shade of deep blue.

Artists use long sticks to stir cloth in dye pits.

Music and Dance

Do you like to beat on a drum? Then Nigeria might be just the place for you. The country has drums in all shapes and sizes. Drummers use their hands or sticks to beat to the music. Drum beats make people want to dance, clap, or tap their feet.

A group of children perform a dance to juju music.

Different groups have their own music, dances, and costumes.
Many dancers put on masks or wear bells around their ankles.
Some even walk on stilts!

A dancer wears a costume for a village festival.

Nigerian girls dance in Lagos.

Story Time

Long before there were books in Nigeria, grandparents taught kids by telling stories. Most of these stories were folktales. They explained where a group of people came from or how the world began.

A nursery school teacher tells children a story.

Storytelling is still alive in Nigeria. These days, many Nigerians write down their stories. Ifeoma Onyefulu writes books that are read by children all over the world. In *A Is for Africa*, she takes each letter of the alphabet and matches it to something in her homeland of Nigeria. What musical instrument do you think goes with *D*?

Mammy Water

"Mammy Water" is a popular folktale from southern Nigeria. A Mammy Water is a mermaid who sings sweet songs to get fishermen to walk into the river. Then, quick as a flash, the Mammy Water steals the man's legs so she can walk on land. Some Nigerians believe that a river changes its direction when a Mammy Water is near.

Chinua Achebe is a famous Nigerian writer.

Soccer Rules!

Nigerians love soccer! As soon as kids start school, they begin to play soccer. School and club soccer teams meet every week or month to play games.

Nigerian boys play soccer in a field. Soccer is called football in Nigeria.

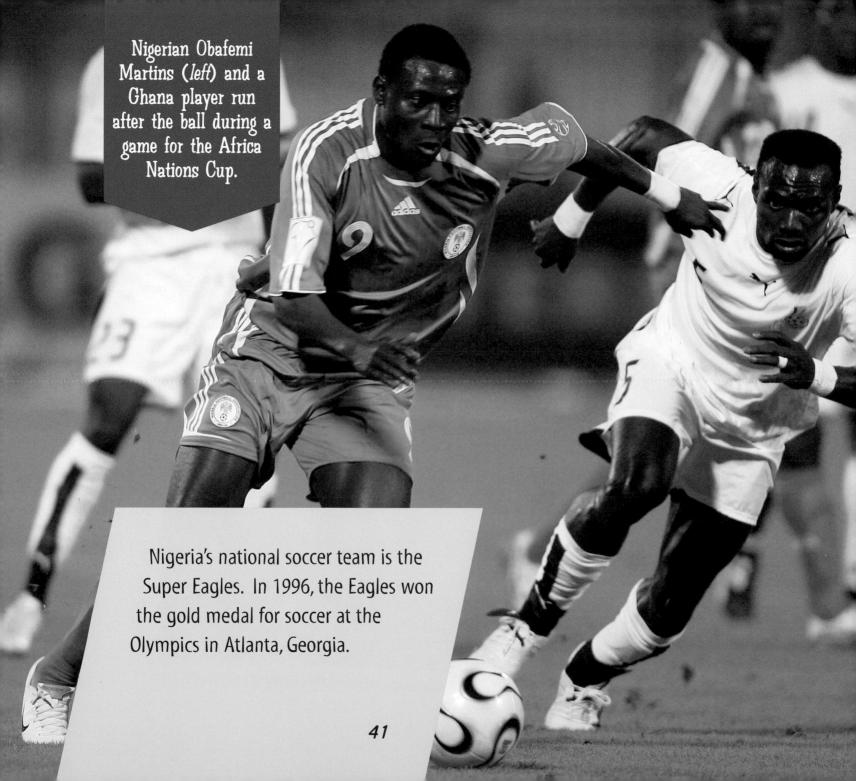

Nigerian Obafemi Martins (*left*) and a Ghana player run after the ball during a game for the Africa Nations Cup.

Nigeria's national soccer team is the Super Eagles. In 1996, the Eagles won the gold medal for soccer at the Olympics in Atlanta, Georgia.

41

Movies and Games

Boom! Pow! Hiss! Splat! Nigerians are big movie fans. They like love stories, adventure movies, and action films. When something sad happens on the screen, the people watching make crying or hissing sounds. During exciting scenes, the audience claps and shouts. Sometimes, people even act as if they are in the movie. They dodge fists or bullets.

A student walks by a wall covered with posters for Nigerian movies.

This board is used to play Ayo.

Nigerians like to play games too. Ayo is popular. It is a traditional Yoruba game. People have played it for many years. Two players move seeds or pebbles around a wooden board. Whoever ends up with the most seeds wins.

THE FLAG OF NIGERIA

Nigeria's flag is green and white. The green stripes stand for the country's agriculture, or farming. The white stripe in the center is for peace and togetherness. Nigerians started using this flag in 1960. That is the year Nigeria became an independent country.

FAST FACTS

FULL COUNTRY NAME: Federal Republic of Nigeria

AREA: 356,669 square miles (923,768 square kilometers), about the size of California, Nevada, and Utah combined

MAIN LANDFORMS: the coast; mangrove swamps; rain forests; the delta Niger Delta; the valley Niger-Benue River Valley; the highlands Jos Plateau; the mountain ranges Shebshi, Mandara, and Gotel; the lakes Kainji and Chad; the savannas Guinea Savanna, Sudan Savanna, and the Sahel

MAJOR RIVERS: Niger River, Benue River

ANIMALS AND THEIR HABITATS: Nile crocodiles, pygmy hippopotamuses, hairy mangrove crabs (swamps, creeks, rivers, delta); drill monkeys, chimpanzees, hornbills (forests); African elephants (forests, savanna); roan antelopes, lions (savanna)

CAPITAL CITY: Abuja

OFFICIAL LANGUAGE: English

POPULATION: about 134,500,000

GLOSSARY

bargain: a talk between a buyer and a seller about the cost of an item. Bargaining ends when both sides agree on a price.

carve: to shape an object from wood or stone

continent: any one of seven large areas of land. The continents are Africa, Antarctica, Asia, Australia, North America, and South America.

delta: a triangle of land that forms where a river enters an ocean

folktale: a story told by word of mouth

gulf: a part of an ocean or sea that reaches into land

mosque: a building where Muslims go to pray

savanna: a tropical grassland with some trees

sculpture: a work of art carved from wood or stone

tropical rain forest: a thick, green forest that gets lots of rain every year

TO LEARN MORE

BOOKS

Brownlie Bojang, Alison. *Nigeria*. Austin, TX: Raintree Steck-Vaughn, 2002. See daily life in Lagos, Nigeria, through the eyes of an eleven-year-old girl.

Echewa, T. Obinkaram. *The Magic Tree: A Folktale from Nigeria*. New York: Morrow Junior Books, 1999. An orphan finds a tree that grants him wishes.

Onyefulu, Ifeoma. *One Big Family: Sharing Life in an African Village*. Toronto: Frances Lincoln, 1996. A Nigerian boy describes what life is like in his village.

Orr, Tamra. *Nigeria*. New York: Children's Press, 2005. Experience Nigeria from A to Z.

Shepard, Aaron. *Master Man: A Tall Tale of Nigeria*. New York: HarperCollins, 2001. Read this Hausa tale about the origin of thunder.

WEBSITES

Motherland Nigeria: Kid Zone
http://www.motherlandnigeria.com/kidzone.html
Check out Boomie O's page of stories, games, pictures, music, jokes, and more.

Nigeria
http://www.timeforkids.com/TFK/hh/go places/main/0,20344,1044380,00.html
This website from the magazine *Time for Kids* features virtual tours of Nigeria, a language page, a quiz, and more.

INDEX